ZEN

The Religion of the Samurai

Julius Evola

Translated, with an Introduction,

by Guido Stucco

Department of Theology,

St. Louis University

Foreword by The Julius Evola

Foundation, Rome

ORIENTAL
CLASSICS

ISBN # 1-55818-329-9

SECOND EDITION,

REVISED

— 2005 —

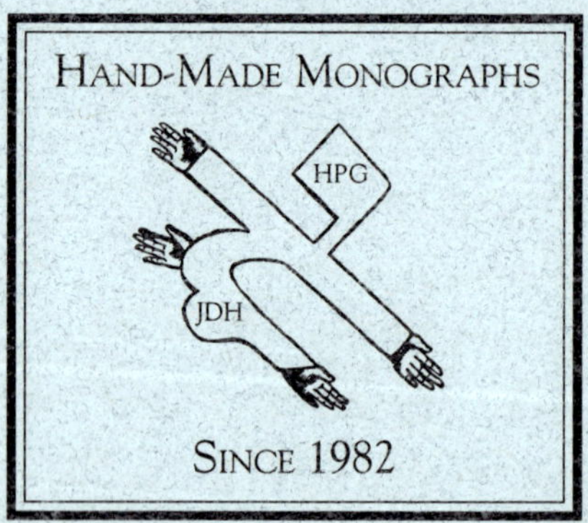

ORIENTAL CLASSICS
HOLMES PUBLISHING GROUP LLC
POSTAL BOX 2370
SEQUIM WA 98382 USA
JDHOLMES.COM

I wish to dedicate this
translation to Chris:

FABER EST SUAE
QUISQUE FORTUNAE

INTRODUCTION

Who was Julius Evola? Considered by many a philosopher, others have cast him in the role of arch-reactionary. Regardless, his philosophical writings have earned him a place as one of the leading representatives of the Traditionalist school.

Like the American poet Ezra Pound before him, the term "fascist" has been accorded Evola for being among the opposition during WWII. For three decades he was shunned by the academic community which took little interest in his writings. Yet Evola has been the object of an interesting revival, acquiring a posthumous revenge of sorts. Conferences and *symposia* devoted to the analysis of his thought have "mushroomed" in the past fifteen years throughout Europe. Secondly, Evola has exercised a magical spell on many people, who having lost faith in so-called progressive ideals, have taken a sharp turn toward Tradition in its quest for something "more transcendent" or for something of a "higher order." These new views cannot be readily found in the wasteland of contemporary society. Thirdly, his spiritual and metaphysical ideas, far from being an appendix to his *Weltanschauung*, represent the very core and can no longer be ignored. Evola's ideas call for a critical analysis and a reasonable response from sympathizers and critics alike.

The reader of these monographs will be able to find detailed information about Julius Evola's life and thought in Richard Drake's writings.[1] This introduction seeks to identify and to characterize the common themes running through all of the following treatises:—*The Path of Enlightenment in the Mithraic Mysteries*; *Zen: The Religion of the Samurai*; *Taoism, The Magic, The Mysticism*; *Rene Guenon: A Teacher for Modern Times.* (Holmes Publishing Group, 1994.) Let us begin with the first theme.

Upon a cursory reading, it is immediately evident that Evola establishes a dichotomy between common, ordinary knowledge, and a secret knowledge which is the prerogative of a selected few. This distinction, also known to Plato, who distinguished between *doxa* and *episteme*, has been the legacy of the Mystery cults, of Mithraism, of Gnosticism, and of all initiatory chains, East or West.

The epistemological distinction between esoteric and exoteric knowledge is rooted, according to Evola, in the ontological classism which separates people, the multitudes, or the *oi polloi,* from the *aristoi*, the heroes, the kings, and the men of knowledge (priests and ascetics). One of the constants in Evola's thought, is his aversion for the empirical subject, who lives, eats, reproduces and dies; everything in his works represents a yearning for something which is more than ordinary existence, more than that condition of life which is heavily conditioned by routines, passions, cravings and superficiality, for what the Germans call *meher als leben* ("more than living"),—a sort of nostalgia for the *Hyperuranium*, for Transcendence, for "what was in the origins." Esotericism is the means to achieve the ultimate reality which all religions strive to achieve, though they call it by many names, as the late Joseph Campbell was fond of saying. During his career as a writer, Julius Evola was involved in an extensive, sophisticated study of esoteric doctrines. In these monographs we find Evola celebrating the metaphysical premises and techniques of Zen and of operative Taoism; elsewhere he sang the praise of Tantrism[2] and of early Buddhism.[3] In another work, commended by Carl G. Jung, he discussed Hermeticism.[4] Scholars of various disciplines will not forgive this controversial and brilliant Italian thinker his incursions in their own fields of competence, such as history, religion, mythology, and psychology. And yet Evola succeeds in weaving a colorful and suggestive pattern, which slowly and gracefully evolves into a well articulated, monolithic *Weltanschauung.*

Another distinctive feature of these works is Julius Evola's firm conviction in the existence of a hierarchy to which all states of being are subject. These states defy the imagination of ordinary people. In the Western religious tradition one does not easily find n articulated cosmology or for that matter a serious emphasis on the soul's experiences in its quest for God. There are the powerful exceptions represented by the writings of St. Bonaventure, St. John of the Cross, Jacob Boehme, St. Theresa of Avila, and other more obscure mystics. Since the personal God of theism is believed to have brought the universe into being, Christianity's focus, in terms of cult and speculation, has shifted from the *cosmos* to its Creator. Evola's knowledge of the Christian tradition was not equal to the erudition he displayed in other subjects. Nevertheless, he attempted to fill what he considered a vacuum in the Christian system. In the monograph dedicated to Mithras he describes the states of being or the spiritual experiences of the initiate to Mithraic mystery tradition and wisdom. These Mithraic experiences are depicted as three-dimensional, heroic, cosmological and esoteric and are juxtaposed to the two-dimensional, devotional, liturgical and exoteric spiritual experiences of formal Christianity. In this work on Zen he celebrates the hierarchical "five grades of merit," through which the initiate grows in wisdom and pursues the personal quest for enlightenment.

A third and final characteristic found in these selections is the rejection of theism and the polemics with Christianity, which in the piece on Guenon is merely outlined (see his comparison of the Christian and the initiatory views of immortality, found in the work on Taoism). His penetrating critique of theism was articulated in the name of "higher" principles and not by an *a priori* hostility to religion and to the concepts of supernatural authority and revelation. What he rejected in theism was the idea of faith, of devotion, of abandonment in a higher power. To faith, he opposed experience; to devotion, heroic and ascetical action; to the God of theism, who is believed to be the ultimate reality, as well as the believer's goal and eschatological hope, Evola opposed the ideal of liberation and of enlightenment as you will find in the examination of Mithraism.

These monographs are a testimony to the restless curiosity and spiritual hunger of a nonspecialist who dared to venture into the domain of scholars and of specialized disciplines, only to extract precious gems of wisdom, unburdened by technical details and *minutiae* which are the obsession of scholars and of university professors. It is my sincere hope that interest in Julius Evola and his ideas will be generated by the translation of these monographs as they represent only a small portion of many untranslated works which have yet to be brought to the attention of the English speaking world.

NOTES

[1] Richard Drake, "Julius Evola and the Ideological Origins of the Radical Right in Contemporary Italy," in *Political Violence and Terror: Motifs and Motivations*, ed., Peter Merkl (Berkeley: University of California Press, 1986), 61-89; "Julius Evola, Radical Fascism and the Lateran Accords," *The Catholic Historical Review* 74 (1988): 403-19; and "The Children of the Sun," chapter in *The Revolutionary Mystique and Terrorism in Contemporary Italy* (Bloomington: Indiana University Press, 1989).

[2] Julius Evola, *The Yoga of Power*, trans. Guido Stucco (Rochester, VT: Inner Traditions, 1992).

[3] Julius Evola, *The Doctrine of the Awakening*, trans. G. Mutton (London: Luzac Co, 1951).

[4] Julius Evola, *The Hermetic Tradition*, trans. E. Rhemus (Rochester, VT: Inner Traditions, 1993).

FOREWORD
Julius Evola Foundation, Rome

In many religions, the material representation of the deity is forbidden. Buddha taught that people should not create an immaterial or mental image of the Absolute. His teaching allowed no foundation from which to argue the existence of a personal God, the creator of the universe. When the Buddha was asked concerning this topic, he answered with a "deafening silence."

Suffering is caused by attachment, not only to material forms, but to mental forms as well. The ultimate purpose of Buddha's teaching was the elimination of suffering through the conscious eradication of attachment, or desire. Until one abandons desire, a person is prone to pass judgment, to be caught up in the polarity of argument or entangled in the net of common opinions.

When the fundamental principle (*dharma*) is realized, one possesses certainty because one *becomes* certainty. This is in accordance with the saying: *Opinions are far away from the vision of the Sublime; certainty is in the vision of the Sublime.* This central tenet of Buddhist Doctrine has nothing in common with mysticism or devotionalism, but rather consists in the disclosure of the path which leads to the knowledge of one's self. Buddha focuses on the effort which the disciple must make, in order to follow the teaching and remove the obstacles to the search. Buddha does not consider divine intervention and requires the apprentice to consider the rising of powers or *siddhis*, which have been awakened by ascetical practices, and which endow him with the ability to perform miraculous feats, to be dangerous developments. The Buddhist texts often portray the ascetic as a warrior, or as a "hero who triumphs in battle," or as the "bull who broke away from all constraints." The Perfected One is like unto a "lone lion." In speaking of himself, Buddha said, "I do not serve anybody, nor need to do so." These proud words have caused many authors to accuse Buddhism of propagating atheism. These authors have either misunderstood the spirit of Buddha's teaching or start from theistic presuppositions, and thus are detractors of Buddha's doctrine. Buddhism should not be analyzed from a religious perspective, because it is not a religion.

Yet Buddha does not deny what he is silent about for he is the one "who has removed the veil." He does not wish other people to see with the eyes of Buddha, but with their own eyes, and he states without complication that, "He who has eyes will see," once the veil has been removed. Buddhism, which is an authentic spiritual path, can be defined as the science of the removal of the veil which covers reality.

Nirvana, which is bliss and supreme reality, does not constitute a distinct reality from those who are in search of it. For man, bliss is a natural state of being, but he is unaware of his true nature. This state of being may be described as the pure light of the Awakening. Strictly speaking, the enlightenment does not consist in the acquisition of something, but it is rather the dissipation of ignorance, which finally allows one to find again what was never lost in the first place. The ascetical effort does not create enlightenment, but rather facilitates it. This enlightenment is none other than the Absolute's self-revelation occurring in the heart of the disciple who opens himself to it. In an ancient text called *Vajracchedika*, Buddha says, "I did not get anything out of the Supreme and perfect enlightenment; this is why it is called *Supreme, perfect enlightenment*."

Zen as a *way* perpetuates the earlier Buddhist tradition. In China, the deeper meaning of Zen is expressed by the term "*wu-shih*," which is simply, *nothing special*. This signifies the original perfect naturalness of the state of enlightenment. Since Zen coincides with the original heart of Buddha's teaching, it cannot be described in a rational way, but can only be lived and realized. Such realization does not concern only ascetical practice, but the ordinary deeds of everyday life as well. A short poem of a *Zenrin* [a community of Zen monks], says: "Sitting quietly, without doing anything; Spring comes and the grass grows by itself."

This is obviously something radically different than praise of inertia or glorification of passive resignation. *Without doing anything* must be understood in the sense of "*acting without acting*" (*wu-wei*), namely, without attachment, since, as it has been remarked, the realization of Buddha's teaching consists in the destruction of attachment. When a Zen *roshi* was asked what was the essence of Zen, he replied: "Eat when you are hungry, drink when you are thirsty and sleep when you are tired."

The ultimate meaning of the Doctrine is behind the apparent banality of this answer. You are to return to a state of perfect spontaneity, in which things happen by themselves, in the right way and at the proper time. Having reached such a state (*satori*), the concepts of birth and death have no meaning, for in the Absolute there is no birth or death. The "*Treatise of the Great Virtue of Wisdom*" says: "All phenomena can be included in two categories: spirit and matter. At a conceptual level we distinguish between spirit and matter, but at the level of the Awakening everything is Spirit... Matter does not exist outside itself."

The *Way* is not attained through concrete thought and analysis, but rather through the practice of meditation, which consists in consciously going beyond one's thought or limitation, a practice in which both mind and body are engaged.

In the Buddhist migration to Japan, Zen (from the Chinese word *chan*, namely concentration, a word which, in turn, was derived from the *Pali* term *dhyana*) was welcomed by the aristocratic warrior class, and thus became the heart and soul of the martial arts. Among these arts, we mention two, *kyu-do* (the art of archery) and *ken-do* (the art of swordsmanship). In these *Ways* (*do* corresponds to the Chinese term *tao*, and is expressed with the same ideogram), the bow and the sword become the vehicles for "active meditation," in which action is the foundation of an eminently spiritual path. Action eventually becomes spontaneous, unhindered, flowing from the remote center of one's being in the perfect harmony of spirit (*ki*), weapon (*ken*, sword) and body *(tai*). When this harmony is achieved, one goes beyond technique, leaving behind hatred as well as love, and one's action becomes irresistible.

Bushido, the Path of the *Samurai*, may be summarized by this statement in Yamamoto Jocho's *Hagakure*: "...to conquer immortality by dying without hesitations." Musashi Miyamoto wrote in The Book of Five Rings, "Beneath the raised sword lies Hell, which you dread; but if you move ahead, you will find the Land of Bliss."

Buddhism as a Way was shown by the prince, Siddhartha Gautama, who belonged to the warrior class of the *Ksatriya*. This Way, from its inception, was strictly reserved for the "noble children of the *Arya*," namely priests and warriors. Buddhism was represented in Japan by the figures of the monk and of the warrior, often combined in the figure of the warrior-monk. This form and representation was also well known in the medieval Western world, e.g., the Knights Templar. Evola in his *The Doctrine of the Awakening*, emphasized the Aryan roots of the Buddhist doctrine in Japan where Zen still preserves and transmits the initiatory contents.

WHAT IS ZEN?

A small book, entitled *Zen and the Art of Archery*, has recently been published by Rigois, a Turin-based publishing house. This precious little book is very revealing of the spiritual foundation of forms, disciplines and behaviors typical of Far Eastern civilizations, particularly those of Japan. The author, Eugen Herrigel, a German professor who taught philosophy in a Japanese university, resolved to study the traditional spirit of Japan in one of its most characteristic expressions, namely Zen. Zen is a Far Eastern school of metaphysics and of Buddhist initiation. As strange as it may first appear, Herrigel was encouraged to learn the traditional art of archery in order to come as close as possible to an understanding of Zen. Herrigel studied this art tirelessly for five years, under the supervision of a master. Herrigel's book describes how his progress in this traditional art and the gradual penetration of the essence of Zen went hand in hand and mutually conditioned each other, eventually producing a deep inner transformation in the author.

It is not easy to briefly summarize and to popularize the contents of this book. As I have said, Zen is an offshoot of Buddhism. It played and still plays an essential role in the formation of Japanese men, especially of the warrior aristocracy, the *samurai*. Buddhism immediately evokes the notion of *nirvana*, which in turn suggests some kind of evanescent and ascetical state of bliss. This is not the case of Zen. *Nirvana*, according to Zen, is a state of inner freedom; a state which is free of the Ego's passions, anxieties and bonds. This state can be preserved in any kind of activity and in any aspect of everyday life. The state of Zen is a different dimension and encompasses life as a whole; it consists of a different way of going through and experiencing life. The "absence of the ego," promoted by Zen, is not the equivalent of apathy or atony; but rather induces a higher form of spontaneity, self-assurance, freedom and calmness during action. It is like one who, after spasmodically grabbing onto something, eventually lets go and in doing so acquires an even higher sense of tranquillity, a higher form of freedom and of security.

Thus, in the Far East there are traditional arts, which, on the one hand, originate from the freedom induced by Zen; on the other hand these arts are, *per se*, ways to achieve this very freedom through training and practice. As odd as it may seem, there is Zen in the art of drama, in the tea ceremony, in the arrangement of flowers, in archery, in wrestling (*judo*), in fencing and so on. All of these arts have a ritual dimension. Besides, in virtue of some inscrutable connections, a complete mastery in one of these arts cannot be achieved without the above-mentioned inner enlightenment and transformation of the sense which one has of his/her own self; this mastery eventually becomes a visible sign of such enlightenment.

Thus Herrigel tells his readers how, in the process of learning the art of archery, slowly and gradually, through the technical problems he encountered in the process of mastering this art, as it is still taught in Japan, he eventually achieved the knowledge and the inner clarification he had been seeking. He realized that archery is not a sport but rather a ritual act and an initiation. In order to be able to master this art, it was necessary for him to eliminate his own Ego, to overcome tensions and to achieve a higher spontaneity. When these conditions were met, the relaxation of his muscles effectively and mysteriously corresponded to maximum strength. The individual, the bow and the target became one; the arrow took off by itself and even without aiming it always reached the target. In these terms, the acknowledgment of his achieved mastery in archery was also the acknowledgment of a higher degree of Zen spirituality. Zen, in this sense, was not a theory or a philosophy, but rather an effective experience and a deeper way of being.

In its description of situations such as these, Herrigel's book is valuable not only because it introduces us to the spirit of an exotic civilization, but also because it enables us to see some of our own Western traditions under a new light. It is known how in older times, and in part, until the Middle Ages, some traditions which were jealously preserved, as well as elements of cults, rituals and even mysteries became associated with various arts. In the past, there were "gods" associated to various arts and rituals of initiation into these arts. The initiation into certain professional and artisan guilds, corporations and *collegia*, was paralleled by a spiritual initiation. As an example, because of the symbolism which characterized it, the art of the medieval stone cutters was the basis of the early Masonry, which drew from it the allegories of the *Opus Magnum*.

Therefore, it is likely that the West knew something similar to what has been preserved until recent times in the Far East in disciplines such as the "way of archery," or the "way of swordsmanship," believed to be identical to the "way of Zen."

The West, due to different presuppositions as far as religious traditions are concerned, may not have experienced this dimension with the same intensity. However, it has known it at another level of existence in which all human activities are reduced to either dull work or to mechanization or to aimless activities, or, at worst, to a soulless sport. All this often ends up strengthening, instead of alleviating, the process of the hardening and of the closing up of the physical Self in modern man.

THE WAY OF THE SAMURAI

The figure of the *samurai* (the members of the Japanese noble warrior class), is well known in the West. Recently, Yukio Mishima's suicide, which he committed to call his people back to the ancient traditions and national pride, has rekindled popular interest in the *samurai*. Little is known regarding the *samurai's* inner traditions. This can be partially explained with the fact that the Japanese are particularly reluctant to talk about their spiritual life. They consider being questioned on such matters almost as a sign which is indicative of a lack of discretion and tact. The Japanese are experts in the art of avoiding the topic, and yet they do so with great courtesy. The increasing modernization, and even Americanization of Japan, is a further negative element when it comes to understanding these traditions.

I would like, at this point, to mention a few things concerning the *samurai's* religion and way of life. The most complete and scholarly source on this matter is a text by Kaiten Nukariya, entitled *The Religion of the Samurai*, (London/Tokyo, 1913). Japan's official religion is Shintoism, a term composed of *shin* (deity) and *do* (way or doctrine). Shintoism thus means, "Doctrine, or way of the Deity." Its basis is faith in the divine origin and mandate of Japan and of its people. Japanese tradition is believed to have originated "from above." This is said to be eminently true in the case of the Japanese imperial dynasty, which assumed a divine character,[1] since it is directly connected with the solar deity, *Amaterasu-o-mikani*. Given these premises, loyalty to Emperor and to nation is believed to be a religious act: country and dynasty have become the concrete reference points of every transcendent act, of every individual *élan* toward what lies beyond mere mortal and finite existence.

The term *matsurigoto* means both government, namely temporal power, and cult, namely the practice of religious affairs. By correspondence, every crime and dishonorable action committed in Japan has taken on the meaning of sacrilege. Thus a crime goes beyond the juridical and social dimensions, and well into the religious dimension.

In Japan, faithfulness and loyalty have not been values restricted to the military and aristocratic elite, but they have rather been extended to include respect for parents; solidarity between relatives or friends; the practice of virtue; respect for the laws; harmony between spouses in the context of a correct hierarchical relationship between the sexes; productivity in the economic sector; work and study; the task of shaping one's character; the safeguard of blood and race. Everything comes down to "faithfulness," and ultimately, to faithfulness to the imperial family. Within this context, any anti-social, immoral, criminal or deviant behavior does not represent the transgression of an abstract rule, or of a more or less insignificant or conventional social "law;" it rather represents betrayal, disloyalty, or a disgrace comparable to that suffered by a warrior who either deserts or fails in his duty toward his superiors. There are no "guilty persons," but rather "traitors," or *beings without honor*; hence the meaning of the famous oriental expression "to lose face," which is considered an intolerable experience.

This is true as far the general atmosphere of traditional Japan is concerned. I will now examine the doctrine which has specifically been the inner soul of the entire caste of the *samurai*, the noble feudal-warrior aristocracy; I am referring to *Zen-shu*, or more simply, Zen. The formative power of such a doctrine has been universally recognized.

The origins of Zen go back to Buddhism. Buddhism became differentiated into the schools of the so-called "Small Vehicle," (*Hinayana*), and the "Great Vehicle," (*Mahayana*). The former had a more empirical and ascetical character; the latter had a more metaphysical inclination. Zen may be considered as a particular expression of *Mahayana*. It originated in the northern regions of India and later moved first to China and then to Japan, where it took a firm hold from 1190 C.E. onwards. Since then, Zen has not ceased to exercise its influence on the Japanese soul in general and more specifically on the warrior class. Such an influence has grown in intensity ever since the Russian-Japanese conflict. It has grown so much, that up to a few years ago it would have been difficult to find a person of noble origins who had not been exposed to Zen views. It is also well known that ascetical training, closely imbued with Zen views, was considered as the natural preparation for those who wished to become officers in the Imperial Army.

Having mentioned the relationship between Zen and Buddhism, somebody may still be perplexed, since in the West Buddhism is thought to be synonymous with alienation from this life. In the West people also think that the Buddhist *nirvana* is the supreme way to evade or to escape from the world, which is equated by Buddhism with suffering, and to take refuge in some kind of shapeless transcendence. It is not necessary, at this point, to describe in detail the essence of Buddhism. It suffices to say that early Buddhism, setting aside the abstract speculations and the ritualism which the Hindu *Brahmin* caste had become obsessed with, focused simply on the issue of "liberation." The truth, which was known even in the ancient Roman world through the words of Sallust: "*omnia orta occidunt et aucta senescunt*," constitutes the starting point of the original Buddhist doctrine. According to this truth, the world is ruled by caducity and impermanence. However, it is possible to escape from this world and to participate in a higher existence which is found beyond life and death. Buddha always avoided talk and "philosophizing." He designated this higher existence with the term *nirvana*, which is not a positive description, but rather an apophatic expression. The term *nirvana* implies that the *conditio sine qua non* which is required to reach that particular state, is the destruction of the craving, thirst, desire, or *fever* which is so operative in human "restlessness." The term *vana* encompasses all of these meanings, while the prefix *nir* refers to the absence of this condition. Thus, to say that this condition is absent does not mean that one has vanished into "nothingness." This is a misconception typical of people who are accustomed to identify life with those qualities, which those who *know* and have a higher insight, consider instead to be fever and obsession.

Zen doctrine essentially takes this orientation again and applies it in a proper context. Zen does not promote involvement in speculation, sacred writings, or canonical texts. This explains its laconic and extremely terse style. According to a famous image, every theory is valid only inasmuch as it points to a path which must be followed using one's own strength. Self-discipline, in almost ascetical yet active terms (though not self-mortifying), constitutes the fundamental element of Zen which was found particularly attractive by the *Samurai*. This self-discipline, though, is very subtle and mostly directed inward. In this discipline one can distinguish the following degrees.

First, it is necessary to master external objects, namely the impressions and the stimuli which emanate from them, and to substitute one's passive attitude toward the objects with an active, dynamic attitude. The disciple is encouraged to realize that every time a yearning leads him toward something, he is not in control of the external object, but rather the object is in control of him. "He who loves a liquor, deceives himself in thinking that he is drinking the liquor; the truth is, the liquor is drinking him." Thus, the goal is to become detached, to find within one's self the one Master. The Western ethics of the Stoics was not dissimilar from this. However, what Zen adds to this detached attitude is the *Mahayana* doctrine of "emptiness," according to which all external objects are, from a metaphysical point of view (*sub species aeternitatis*), nothing else but illusory projections. These projections are given an appearance of reality and power by our own cravings.

In the second stage, one has to master the body, and affirm one's authority over the entire physical organism. It has been said: "Imagine your own body as something other than yourselves. If it cries, quiet it right away, as a strict mother does with her own child. If it is capricious, control it as a rider does his own horse, through the bridle. If it is sick, administer medicines to it, just as a doctor does with a patient. If it disobeys you, punish it, as a teacher does with a pupil." This should become a discipline marked by habit and not remain a mere theory. It must become practice. Quite often at this level, the spiritual exercise complements military training. In ancient times there were "competitions of resoluteness," which determined who, among the disciples, knew how to endure for the longest time the worst heat during the summer and the most glacial cold during the winter.

Generally speaking, it is typical of Zen to look upon various "martial arts," including other arts, as some kind of spiritual and even initiatory counterpart. Zen even views the mastery of a given art as some kind of external sign of a corresponding inner realization.

The third stage consists in the control of the passions and emotions and in the achievement of an inner equilibrium. One must realize the irrationality and the futility of all fears, hopes, and excitements, and eventually "bring the heart under control." In regard to this, there is an anecdote about O-yo-mei, the commander in chief of an army who was fighting a decisive struggle against an attempted usurpation. In the course of the military campaign he did not neglect to practice Zen in his own headquarters. When he was told that his troops had been routed, his staff panicked, but O-yo-mei did not get upset, but gave some brief instructions. A little later the news arrived that, in a further development of the battle, victory had been won. O-yo-mei remained as calm as before and did not interrupt his Zen practice. What must be emphasized is that Zen does not promote a stiff insensibility, but rather that it attempts to remove any useless feeling and any needless distress. Another example is provided by the *kamikaze*, the pilots who embarked on suicide missions during WWII. These people, almost all of whom practiced Zen, were capable of attending to their duties and even to have fun, even though they knew that at any given time they could be asked to fly a mission without hope of returning.

The fourth stage implies the "rejection of the Ego." Not only is it necessary to stop feeling "important," but also to believe that one's individual existence is real. The attachment to the Ego is the most difficult bond to rescind; only then one will arrive at the threshold of an "enlightened consciousness," which is synonymous with a state of super-individuality and of active impersonality. In fact, this higher dimension, which, in a certain sense could also be characterized as "contemplation," is not associated with a withdrawn and cloistered life, but is rather understood as a state of consciousness which should be permanent and thus permeate every experience or activity. There is a saying: "To be attached to no thing is contemplation; if you understand this, you will never cease to contemplate, even as you go, stay, sit or lay down."

From another perspective, a distinction is made between five degrees of discipline, the so-called *Ko-kun-go-i*, namely the "five degrees of merit."

The first degree is the "level of revulsion," which corresponds to the disciple who turns from the outer to the inner world, escaping the domination of the former. A special allegory is employed: the higher Self, to which one aspires, is represented as sovereign, whom one serves as a subject. Second, comes the "level of service," characterized by loyalty toward this inner Master and by a constant "service," characterized by obedience, affection, fear to offend, just as it is expected from a king's personal attendant. What follows is the "level of valor," which must be displayed in fighting, routing and subjugating a rebel army of passions and instincts which has risen up against its king. At this level one is promoted from personal attendant to general. The fourth level is the "level of cooperation." One does not merely fight and "defend the Center," but joins the ranks of those who advise the "sovereign" about State affairs and social order. The last level is called the "level of super-merit," (*Ko-ko*) and it is the dwelling place of the sovereign himself, with whom one identifies. At this stage, all actions cease, and the spiritual sovereignty and state of consciousness characterized by a higher freedom, are finally realized.

The symbolic or allegorical representation of the various stages of spiritual discipline, as it is practiced in Zen, is very important, because it can act as liaison between the inner domain and the outer world; in other words, it shows how Zen succeeded in becoming incorporated into the official Shintoist religion of Japan, which, as I have said, had as its cornerstone the cult of the Emperor. We can say that the *samurai* projected onto the Emperor his own spiritual ideal; in the Emperor the *samurai* saw the symbolic "sovereign" I have just described in the allegory of the five levels of merit. In this way, at least in principle, a parallelism was established between the spiritual and the political discipline of an elite. This parallelism was able to bestow a higher meaning on everything that is active commitment, service, struggle, sacrifice, knowledge and wisdom for the welfare and the power of the community, of which the Emperor (*Tenno*) was the apex.

All of this took on a "ritual" value for the *samurai*, as well as a value of a path of inner realization. Thus, even the supreme sacrifice of one's life for the sake of the nation, was considered by the *samurai* as the sacrifice of the ephemeral and limited part of himself in favor of the "Higher Self," which participates in the so-called "Great Liberation."

These examples will hopefully shed some light on the meaning of the way of the *samurai*. A careful reader will notice some correspondence with orientations which even the West knew once, although in different forms. It will suffice here to mention the ascetical-martial ideal of the medieval orders of knights; the value given during the Middle Ages to "faithfulness," so much that it became a sacrament of sorts as well as the criterion to discriminate ontologically between human beings. From this imperial ideal, there flowed the transcendent and sacred justifications which the *Ghibellins* enunciated, when they referred to a mysterious "royal religion of Melchizedek."

A few years ago Japan loomed, in the modern world, as a unique and marvelous example of a civilization in which the jealous preservation of traditional secular ideas went hand in hand with a high degree of modernization of the external structures. Unfortunately, following Japan's collapse in WWII, this equilibrium was broken, and the energies of the Yamato race, namely the Japanese, have been invested in the re-edification of the external world. The result has been an "economic miracle" which has placed Japan among the main industrial and economic super-powers; in the meantime, especially in the great cities, life and customs have been contaminated to a high degree, and without much regret, by modern Western influences, especially by American ones. This contamination can easily be seen in movies and in various documentaries.

Yukio Mishima's bloody act, his *hara-kiri*, should have impressed the meaning of "Awaken, Japan!," analogous to "*Deutschland, erwache!*" which had been a rallying cry in central Europe following WWI. Sadly, Mishima's gesture has just been considered an oddity, and some even called it "theatrical." If modern developments continue their course, Mishima's death will only be a distant memory of the past and never be seen in a proper light, namely as an example of high paradigmatic value. But again, this will be yet another sign of the general and unstoppable advent of an era, which even in times of old, had been foreseen and described in terms of a "dark age": the *Kali-yuga*.

THE MEANING AND CONTEXT OF ZEN

We know the kind of interest Zen has evoked even outside specialized disciplines, since being popularized in the west by D.T. Suzuki through his books *Introduction to Zen Buddhism* and *Essays in Zen Buddhism*. These works have also been translated into French. This popular interest is due to the paradoxical encounter between East and West. The ailing West perceives that Zen has something "existential" and surrealistic to offer. Zen's notion of a spiritual realization, free from any faith and any bond, not to mention the mirage of an instantaneous and somehow gratuitous "spiritual breakthrough," capable of relieving all existential anguishes, has exercised a fascinating attraction on many Westerners. However, this is true, for the most part, only superficially. There is a considerable difference between the spiritual dimension of the "philosophy of crisis," which has become popular in the West as a consequence of its materialistic and nihilist development, and the spiritual dimension of Zen, which has been rooted in the spirituality of the Buddhist tradition. Any true encounter between Zen and the West, presupposes, in a Westerner, either an exceptional predisposition, or the capability to operate a *metanoia*. By *metanoia* I mean an inner turnabout, affecting not so much one's intellectual "attitudes," but rather a dimension which in every time and in every place has been conceived as a deeper reality.

Zen was a secret doctrine and not to be found in scriptures. It was passed on by the Buddha to his disciple Mahakassapa. This secret doctrine was introduced in China around the sixth century C.E. by Bodhidharma (see cover illustration). The canon was transmitted in China and Japan through a succession of teachers and "patriarchs." In Japan it is a living tradition and has many advocates and numerous *Zendos* ("Halls of Meditation.")

As far as the spirit informing the tradition is concerned, Zen may be considered as a continuation of early Buddhism. Buddhism arose as a vigorous reaction against the theological speculation and the shallow ritualism into which the ancient Hindu priestly caste had degraded after possessing a sacred, lively wisdom since ancient times. Buddha made *tabula rasa* of all this: he focused instead on the practical problem of how to overcome what in the popular mind is referred to as "life's suffering." According to esoteric teachings, this suffering was considered as the state of caducity, restlessness, 'thirst' and forgetfulness typical of ordinary people. Having followed the path leading to spiritual awakening and to immortality without anyone's help, Buddha pointed the way to those who felt an attraction to it. It is well known that Buddha is not a name, but an attribute or a title meaning "the awakened One," "He who has achieved enlightenment," or "the awakening." Buddha was silent about the content of his experience, since he wanted to discourage people from assigning to speculation and philosophizing a primacy over action. Therefore, unlike his predecessors, he did not talk about *Brahman* (the absolute), or about *Atman* (the transcendental Self), but only employed the term *nirvana*, at the risk of being misunderstood. Some, in fact, thought, in their lack of understanding, that *nirvana* was to be identified with the notion of "nothingness," an ineffable and evanescent transcendence, almost bordering on the limits of the unconscious and of a state of unaware non-being.

So, in a further development of Buddhism, what occurred again, *mutatis mutandis*, was exactly the situation against which Buddha had reacted; Buddhism became a religion, complete with dogmas, rituals, scholasticism and mythology. It eventually became differentiated into two schools: *Mahayana* and *Hinayana*. The former was more grandiose in metaphysics and eventually grew complacent with its abstruse symbolism. The teachings of the latter school were more strict and to the point, and yet too concerned about the mere moral discipline, which became increasingly monastic. Thus the essential and original nucleus, namely the esoteric doctrine of the enlightenment, was almost lost.

At this crucial time Zen appeared, declaring the uselessness of these so-called methods and proclaiming the doctrine of *satori* . *Satori* is a fundamental inner event, a sudden existential breakthrough, corresponding in essence to what I have called the "awakening." But this formulation was new and original and it constituted a radical change in approach. *Nirvana*, which had been variously considered as the alleged Nothingness, as extinction, and as the final end result of an effort aimed at obtaining liberation (which according to some may require more than one lifetime), now came to be considered as the *normal human condition*. By these lights, every person has the nature of Buddha and every person is already liberated, and therefore, situated above and beyond birth and death. It is only necessary to become aware of it, to realize it, *to see within one's nature*, according to Zen's main expression. *Satori* is like a timeless opening up. On the one hand, *satori* is something sudden and radically different from all the ordinary human states of consciousness; it is like a catastrophic trauma within ordinary consciousness. On the other hand, *satori* is what leads one back to what, in a higher sense, should be considered as normal and natural; thus, it is the exact opposite of an *ecstasis*, or trance. It is the rediscovery and the appropriation of one's true nature: it is the enlightenment which draws out of ignorance or out of the subconscious the deep reality of what was and will always be, regardless of one's condition in life.

The consequence of *satori* is a completely new way to look at the world and at life. To those who have experienced it, everything is the same (things, other beings, one's self, "heaven, the rivers and the vast earth"), and yet everything is fundamentally different. It is as if a new dimension was added to reality, transforming its meaning and value. According to the Zen Masters, the essential characteristic of the new experience is the overcoming of every dualism: of the inner and outer; the I and not-I; of finitude and infinity; being and non-being; appearance and reality; "empty" and "full"; substance and accidents. Another characteristic is that any value posed by the finite and confused consciousness of the individual, is no longer discernible. And thus, the liberated and the non-liberated, the enlightened and the non-enlightened, are yet one and the same thing. Zen effectively perpetuates the paradoxical equation of *Mahayana* Buddhism, *nirvana=samsara,* and the Taoist saying "the return is infinitely far." It is as if Zen said: liberation should not be looked for in the next world; this very world is the next world; it is liberation and it does not need to be liberated. This is the point of view of *satori,* of perfect enlightenment, of "transcendent wisdom" (*prajnaparamita*).

Basically, this consciousness is a shift of the self's center. In any situation and in any event of ordinary life, including the most trivial ones, the ordinary, dualistic and intellectual sense of one's self is substituted with the sense of a being who no longer perceives an "I" opposed to a "non-I", and who transcends and overcomes any antithesis. This being eventually comes to enjoy a perfect freedom and incoercibility. He is like the wind, which blows where it wills, and like a naked being which is everything and possesses everything because he has let go and abandoned everything, embracing poverty.

Zen, or at least mainstream Zen, emphasizes the discontinuous, sudden and unpredictable character of *satori* disclosure. In regard to this, Suzuki was at fault when he took issue with the techniques used in Hindu schools such as *Samkya* and *Yoga.* These techniques were also contemplated in early Buddhist texts. Suzuki employed the simile of water, which in a moment turns into ice. He also used the simile of an alarm, which, as a consequence of some vibration, suddenly goes off. There are no disciplines, techniques or efforts, according to Suzuki, which by themselves may lead one to *satori.* On the contrary, it is claimed that *satori* often occurs spontaneously, when one has exhausted all the resources of his being, especially the intellect and logical faculty of understanding. In some cases *satori* is said to be facilitated by violent sensations and even by physical pain. Its cause may be the mere perception of an object as well as any event in ordinary life, provided a certain latent predisposition exists in the subject.

Regarding this, some misunderstandings may occur. Suzuki acknowledged that "generally speaking, there are no specific indications on the inner work preceding *satori.*" However, he talked about the necessity of first going through "a true baptism of fire." After all, the very institution of the so-called "Halls of Meditation" (*Zendo*), where those who strive to obtain *satori* submit themselves to a regimen of life which is partially analogous to that of some Catholic religious orders, bespeaks the necessity of a preliminary preparation. This preparation may last for several years. The essence of Zen seems to consist in a maturation process, identical to the one in which one almost reaches a state of an acute existential instability. At that point, the slightest push is sufficient to produce a change of state, a spiritual breakthrough, the opening which leads to the "intuitive vision of one's nature." The Masters know the moment in which the mind of the disciple is mature and ready to open up; it is then that they eventually give the final, decisive push. This push may sometimes consist of a simple gesture, an exclamation, in something apparently irrelevant, or even illogical and absurd. This suffices to induce the collapse of the false notion of individuality. Thus, *Satori* replaces this notion with the "normal state," and one assumes the "original face, which one had before creation." One no longer "chases after echoes" and "shadows." This, under some aspects, brings to mind the existential theme of "failure," or of "being shipwrecked" (*das Scheitern*, in Kierkegaard and in Jaspers). In fact, as I have mentioned, the opening often takes place when all the resources of one's being have been exhausted and one has his back against the wall. This can be seen in relation to some practical teachings methods used by Zen. The most frequently employed methods, on an intellectual plane, are the *koan* and the *mondo*. The disciple is confronted with a saying or with questions which are paradoxical, absurd and sometimes even grotesque and "surrealistic." He must labor with his mind, if necessary for years, until he has reached the extreme limit of all his normal faculties of comprehension. Then, if he dares proceed further on that road, he may find catastrophe, but if he can turn the situation upside down, he may achieve *metanoia*. This is the point where *satori* is usually achieved.

Zen's norm is that of absolute autonomy; no gods, no cults, no idols. To literally empty oneself of everything, including God. "If you meet Buddha on the road, kill him," a saying goes. It is necessary to abandon everything, without leaning on anything, and then to proceed forward, with one's essence, until the crisis point is reached. It is very difficult to say more about *satori*, or to compare it with various forms of initiatory mystical experience whether Eastern or Western. One is supposed to spend only the training period in Zen monasteries. Once the disciple has achieved *satori*, he returns to the world, choosing a way of life that fits his need. One may think of *satori* as a form of transcendence which is brought into immanence, as a natural state, in every form of life.

The behavior which proceeds from the newly acquired dimension, which is added to reality as a consequence of *satori*, may well be summarized by Lao-Tzu's expression: "To be whole in the part." In regard to this, it is important to realize the influence which Zen has exercised on the Far-Eastern way of life. Zen has been called "the samurai's philosophy," and it has also been said that "the way of Zen is identical to the way of archery," or to the "way of the sword." This means that any activity in one's life, may be permeated by Zen and thus be elevated to a higher meaning, to a "wholesomeness" and to an "impersonal activity." This kind of activity is based on a sense of the individual's irrelevance, which nevertheless does not paralyze one's actions, but which rather confers calm and detachment. This detachment, in turn, favors an absolute and "pure" undertaking of life, which in some cases reaches extreme and distinct forms of self-sacrifice and heroism, inconceivable to the majority of Westerners (e.g., the *kamikaze* in WWII).

Thus, what C.G. Jung claims is simply ridiculous, namely that Psychoanalysis, more than any other Western school of thought, is capable of understanding Zen. According to Jung, *satori* coincides with the state of wholeness, devoid of complexes or inner splitting, which psychoanalytic treatment claims to achieve whenever the intellect's obstructions and its sense of superiority are removed, and whenever the conscious dimension of the soul is reunited with the unconscious and with "Life." Jung failed to realize that the methods and presuppositions of Zen, are exactly the opposite of his own. There is no "unconscious," as a distinct entity, to which the conscious has to be reconnected; Zen speaks of a super-conscious vision (enlightenment, *bodhi* or "awakening"), which actualizes the "original and luminous nature" and which, in so doing, destroys the unconscious. It is possible though, to notice similarities between Jung's views and Zen's, since they both talk about the feeling of one's "totality" and freedom which is manifested in every aspect of life. However, it is important to explain the level at which these views appear to coincide.

Once Zen found its way to the West, there was a tendency to "domesticate" and to moralize it, playing down its potential radical and "antinomian" (namely, antithetical to current norms) implications, and by emphasizing the standard ingredients which are held so dear by "spiritual" people, namely love and service to one's neighbor, even though these ingredients have been purified in an impersonal and non-sentimental form. Generally speaking, there are many doubts on the "practicability" of Zen, considering that the "doctrine of the awakening" has an initiatory character.

Thus, it will only be able to inspire a minority of people, in contrast to later Buddhist views, which took the form of a religion open to everyone, or of a code of mere morality. As the re-establishment of the spirit of early Buddhism, Zen should have remained an esoteric doctrine. It has been so as we can see by examining the legend concerning its origins. However, Suzuki himself was inclined to give a different account; he emphasized those aspects of *Mahayana* which "democratize" Buddhism (after all, the term *Mahayana* has been interpreted to mean "Great Vehicle," even in the sense that it extends to wider audiences, and not just to a few elect). If one was to fully agree with Suzuki, some perplexities on the nature and on the scope of *satori* may arise; more specifically one should ask whether such an experience merely affects the psychological, moral or mental domain, or whether it affects the ontological domain, as is the case of every authentic initiation. In that event, it can only be the privilege of a very restricted number of people.

NOTE

[1] This century-old belief, deeply rooted in the Japanese people, has been shaken only after the defeat which Japan suffered in WWII.

For a Complete List of Publications,
Please address:
Holmes Publishing Group LLC
Postal Box 2370
Sequim WA 98382 USA
Secure Orders:
jdholmes.com